The MAILBOX®
The Education Center®

grades
A–K

NUMBERS
for Little Learners

Over 90 Simple Activities to Build Number Sense Throughout the Early Childhood Day!

- Counting to 5, 10, 12, and 20
- One-to-one correspondence
- Counting backward from 10 to 1
- Recognizing and naming numerals
- Ordering numerals

- Identifying missing numbers
- Writing numerals
- Comparing sets
- Matching sets to numerals
- Sequencing ordinal numbers

Plus Ten More Essential Number Skills

Written by Ada Goren

Managing Editor: Allison Ward

Editorial Team: Becky S. Andrews, Kimberley Bruck, Karen P. Shelton, Diane Badden, Thad H. McLaurin, Sharon Murphy, Karen A. Brudnak, Juli Docimo Blair, Hope Rodgers, Dorothy C. McKinney

Production Team: Lori Z. Henry, Pam Crane, Rebecca Saunders, Jennifer Tipton Cappoen, Chris Curry, Sarah Foreman, Theresa Lewis Goode, Greg D. Rieves, Barry Slate, Donna K. Teal, Zane Williard, Tazmen Carlisle, Marsha Heim, Lynette Dickerson, Mark Rainey

Includes 8 Reproducible Take-Home Booklets!

www.themailbox.com

©2006 The Mailbox®
All rights reserved.
ISBN10 #156234-699-7 • ISBN13 #978-156234-699-7

Manufactured in the United States
10 9 8 7 6 5 4 3 2 1

Table of Contents

How to Use This Book

Quickly find just the activity you're looking for:

"I need my students to practice a specific skill."

1. Look at the skills grid on page 3.
2. Find the skill you want students to practice.
3. Scan across to find the pages featuring activities on that skill.

"I want to incorporate math into different times of the day."

1. Look at the skills grid on page 3.
2. Find the component of the day, such as circle time, songs and fingerplays, or centers.
3. Scan down to find the skills covered in that section's activities.

Skills Grid

	Circle Time	Songs and Fingerplays	Centers	Snack Time	Arts and Crafts	Booklets
number awareness						64
understanding one-to-one correspondence			26	40	48	
counting to 3	4	16	26	40	48	
counting to 5	4	16	27	41	49	68
counting to 10	8	17	27		49	71
counting to 12						74
counting to 20	8	17	28	41	50	77
counting backward from 10 to 1	9	18		42	51	80
recognizing written numbers 11 to 20		21				
recognizing and naming written numbers to 10	5	18	28	42	51	
recognizing and naming written numbers 11 to 20			29		52	
identifying written numbers 1 to 10	10	19				
identifying written numbers 11 to 20	10					
forming numbers	6		32	43, 44		
writing numbers 1 to 10			31		54	87
writing numbers 11 to 20					55	
identifying missing numbers to 10	12	19	30			
ordering numbers to 5	11			43	52	
ordering numbers to 10		20	29		53	
ordering numbers to 20	11		30			
identifying ordinal numbers		22			56	
sequencing ordinal numbers	12		34	45		
comparing sets to 10	5	20				
comparing sets	6		32	44	55	83
matching sets to numerals	7	22	33	45	56	
understanding the concept of zero	7	21			53	

Circle Time

Roll, Count, and Move!
Counting to 3

To prepare for this energetic activity, wrap a cubic tissue box in plain paper and program each of the sides, using the numbers 1, 2, and 3. (Each number will be used twice.) During circle time, announce a movement for the class to perform, such as jumping jacks, toe touches, or hops. Then have a volunteer roll the cube and announce the number that lands face up. Have little ones perform the featured movement the corresponding number of times as they count in unison. To begin the next round of play, invite a student to name a movement and roll the cube. Continue as desired to keep your students' math skills rolling along.

Two jumping jacks!

One!

Round and Round
Counting to 5

Who will be the last one standing in this counting game? Try it and see! Have students stand in a circle. Announce a target number from two to five. Then have students count off around the circle, beginning with the number one, until the target number is reached. The child that calls out the target number sits down, and the next child begins counting from one again. The game continues in this manner until only one child is standing. Invite the last child standing to choose the target number for the next round of play.

Four!

The Number-Pokey
Recognizing and naming numbers

Put a numerical twist on a favorite song and dance! Have students stand in a circle and give each child a number card. (If desired, use the patterns on pages 103–112.) Next, lead students in the song shown. At the end of the verse, invite each student holding the indicated number to raise his card and shout the name of his number. Then sing the song again, substituting a different number. Continue in this manner until each child has a turn.

(sung to the tune of "The Hokey-Pokey")

You put your number in.
You put your number out.
You put your number in and you shake it all about!
You do the Number-Pokey,
And you turn yourself around.
If you have this number, shout! [Four]!

Take Aim!
Comparing sets to 10

Place two plastic hoops on the floor in the center of your circle. Give each of up to ten students a beanbag and have each child take a turn tossing her beanbag into the hoop of her choice. Next, have students count the beanbags in each hoop. Enlist students' help to compare the sets. Which has more? Which has fewer? Are the sets equal? Repeat the activity with a different group of students for additional set comparison practice.

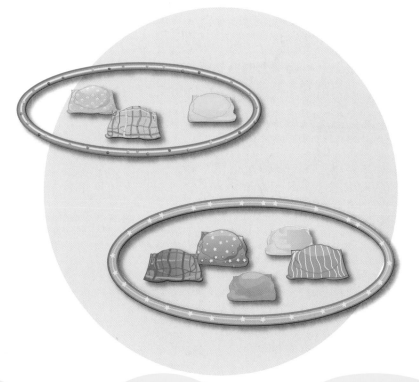

Treasure Hunt
Comparing sets

Shiver me timbers—youngsters are sure to find this activity engaging! While students are out of the room, hide ten to 20 yellow construction paper circles (gold pieces) in your classroom. During circle time, divide your class into two teams. Present each team with an empty box to represent a treasure chest and then explain that each team will hunt for gold pieces. When a child finds a gold piece, she puts it in her team's treasure chest. Set a time limit, such as three minutes, and encourage students to find as many gold pieces as possible. At the end of the designated time, have everyone return to the circle. Lead students in counting the gold pieces in each chest and then comparing the two sets. Which set has fewer? Which set has more? Are the sets equal?

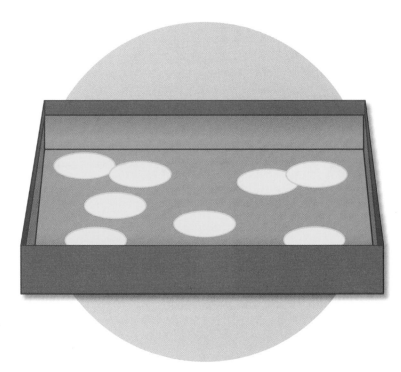

Follow the Arrows
Forming numbers

Numeral formation practice is just a step away with this activity! In advance, use masking tape to outline a large numeral on the floor of your circle-time area. Place a colorful sticky dot on the starting point and then draw arrows on the tape to show the direction of the writing strokes. Gather youngsters and introduce the numeral. Then chant the rhyme shown as each child takes a turn following the arrows as he walks on the taped number. If desired, repeat the activity another day with a different number.

Follow the arrows.
Stay on the line!
You'll make a number [5].
Doesn't it look fine?

Making Sandwiches
Matching numbers to sets

To prepare, copy the bread-slice patterns on page 13 to make a class supply. Cut out the slices; then color half brown (to resemble peanut butter) and half purple (to resemble jelly). Program the back of each peanut butter slice with a different number. Program the back of each jelly slice with a dot set that corresponds to one of the numbers.

At circle time, give each child a slice. Then, at your signal, have youngsters search for the child holding the corresponding slice. When a student finds her match, the two youngsters sit down together and make a sandwich from their slices. After all the sandwiches are made, confirm each twosome's match. Then redistribute the slices for another round of play.

The Zero Jar
Understanding the concept of zero

Show youngsters an empty plastic jar. Tell students that everyone will add a special number of items to the jar, and that special number is zero! Explain that since *zero* means *none*, students can pick any item they wish to place in the jar. Then sing the song shown, inserting your name and item where indicated. Then sing the song again as you pass the jar to the child next to you, who names an item at the appropriate time. Have youngsters continue passing the jar around the circle until every child has put zero items in the jar!

(sung to the tune of "The Farmer in the Dell")

Zero in the jar,
Zero in the jar,
[Ms. Page] put zero [trains] inside!
Zero in the jar!

Pass the Cookies
Counting to 10

Serve up counting practice—fresh from the bakery! Store ten tagboard circles (cookies) in a paper bag. During circle time, pass the bag around the circle as you recite the rhyme shown. At the end of the rhyme, have the child holding the bag open it and take out one cookie as she says, "One." She passes the bag to the next child who takes out another cookie and says, "Two." Youngsters continue passing and counting until the bag is empty and the group determines the total number of cookies. Then collect the cookies, secretly place a different amount in the bag, and play another round!

Cookies, cookies,
Freshly baked.
How many cookies,
Did we take?

Eight!

Number Path
Counting to 20

Get little ones on the path to moving and counting! Place 20 large index cards in a path on the floor in an open area; then adhere them to the floor with clear Con-Tact covering. During circle time, ask each youngster to first walk the path, quietly counting aloud as she steps onto each card. Then have students travel the path again, this time jumping on each card as they count aloud. Repeat the activity with different movements as desired.

3, 2, 1...Popcorn!
Counting backward from 10 to 1

Youngsters pretend to pop popcorn during this group activity. Give each child a handful of white packing peanuts. Set an imaginary timer and then lead students in a countdown from the number ten. When students reach the number one, encourage them to shout, "Popcorn!" and toss their packing peanuts into the air. Then enlist students' help to scoop up the popcorn and pop it again!

Ten Little Frogs
Counting backward from 10 to 1

In advance, make a green construction paper copy of the frog cards on page 14. Cut apart the cards and place them in a pocket chart. During circle time, recite the first verse of the poem shown. At the end, invite a volunteer to remove a frog from the chart, ribbiting as she returns to her spot in the circle. Then lead youngsters in repeating the poem, substituting the new number of frogs. Continue in this manner until there are no frogs left. Then recite the last verse. For added fun, invite youngsters to hop like frogs at the end of the poem.

[Ten] little frogs on a sunny day.
One got up and hopped away!

Last verse:
No little frogs on a sunny day.
Can you be like them and hop away?

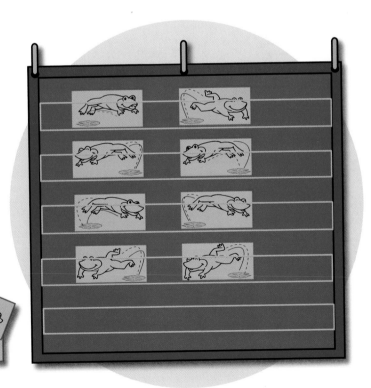

Pass the Presents
Identifying written numbers 1 to 10

Gather ten lidded boxes and, if desired, attach a bow to the lid of each. Program the inside of each box with a different number from one through ten. At circle time, play some lively music and pass the presents around the circle. After a few moments, stop the music and ask each child, in turn, to open her box and identify the number inside. Then have her replace the lid. Restart the music and have students pass the presents for more numeral-recognition practice.

Numbers in the Mail
Identifying written numbers 11 to 20

Deliver first-class number identification practice with this activity! On each of a class supply of blank postcards or index cards, write a number from 11 through 20. Store the postcards in a bag that resembles a mailbag. At circle time, invite a student to carry the mailbag as he pretends to be a mail carrier and delivers one postcard to each child. Next, have each child, in turn, identify the number written on her postcard. Once students have named their numbers, collect the postcards and then play again with a different mail carrier.

5 • 6 • 7 • 8 • 9 • 0 • 1 • 2 • 3 • 4 • 5 • 6 • 7 • 8 • 9 • 0 • 1 • 2 • 3 • 4 • 5 • 6 • 7

Flashlight Fun
Ordering numbers to 5

Use the number cards on pages 103–105 for this bright idea! Display the numbers one through five in random order. Recite the poem below; then help a student volunteer arrange the numbers in correct order. Once the numbers are in place, hand him a flashlight, dim the classroom lights, and invite him to shine the flashlight beam on each consecutive number as the class counts aloud. Then rearrange the number cards and repeat the activity with another volunteer.

These numbers are mixed up!
These numbers aren't right!
Put them all in order,
And then shine the light!

Build a Caterpillar
Ordering numbers to 20

This cute caterpillar grows as youngsters sequence numbers. In advance, draw a cute caterpillar face on a paper circle and display it within student reach on a wall. Also program 20 colorful paper circles with a different number from one through 20. During circle time, randomly distribute the circles and ask youngsters to complete the caterpillar's body by attaching the numbers in order behind the head. Provide each child with a rolled piece of tape as he adds his circle to the wall. Then enlist students' help to count aloud to 20 using the completed caterpillar as a guide.

Bye-Bye, Butterfly!
Identifying missing numbers to 10

Make five copies of the butterfly pattern on page 15; then laminate them and cut them out. Use a wipe-off marker to program each butterfly with a different number in a sequence. Display the butterflies in numerical order in a pocket chart. To begin, recite the poem below, asking youngsters to cover their eyes when indicated. Remove one butterfly from the chart and conceal it. Then have youngsters study the chart and determine which number is missing. When a child correctly identifies the number, return the butterfly. Then invite that youngster to secretly remove a butterfly during the next round of play.

Five little butterflies, flying high.
When you're not looking,   *(Cover eyes.)*
One says, "Bye-bye!"

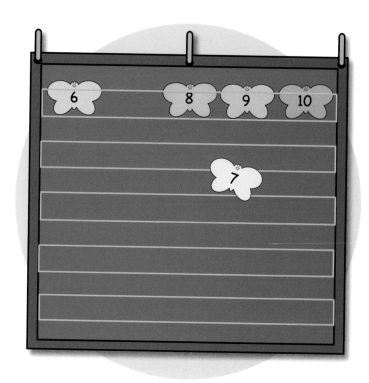

Slide Into Ordinals
Sequencing ordinal numbers

Take circle time to the playground for a fun exploration of ordinal numbers! Ask five children to line up at the slide while the rest of the group watches. Have those students slide down one at a time while you and the students count from one to five. Then explain that you can also identify the sliders with numbers that tell the order in which they slid. Have each child in the group slide again, this time using ordinal numbers to count the sliders. Repeat the activity with a new group of students until everyone has had a turn.

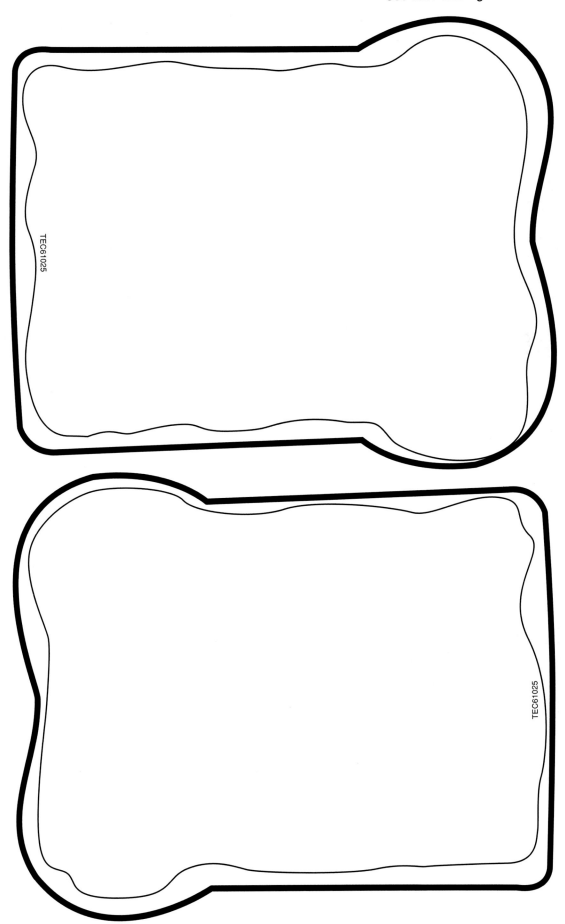

TEC61025

TEC61025

Frog Patterns
Use with "Ten Little Frogs" on page 9.

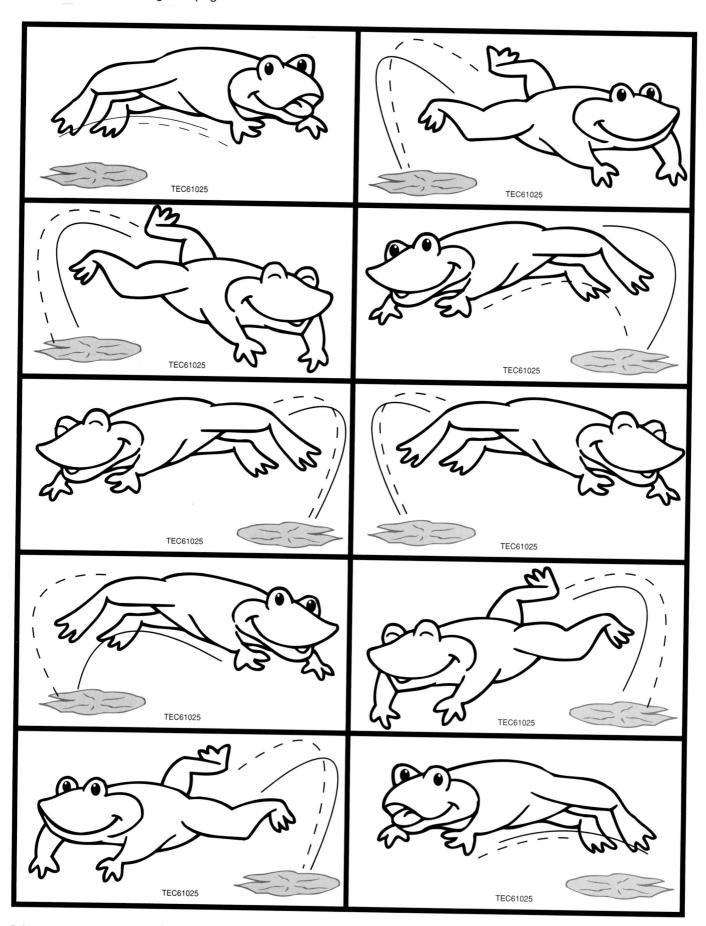

TEC61025

TEC61025

Songs & Fingerplays

`9 • 0 • 1 • 2 • 3 • 4`

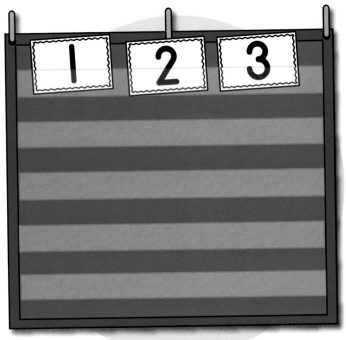

Three Little Numbers
Counting to 3

Little ones will want to sing this cheerful song again and again! Place number cards 1, 2, and 3 in order in a pocket chart. (If desired, use the cards on pages 103 and 104.) Then point to the numbers repeatedly as you lead students in the song.

(sung to the tune of "Ten Little Indians")

One little, two little, three little numbers.
One little, two little, three little numbers.
One little, two little, three little numbers.
Count them now with me!
(Slowly count to three.)

I Knew You Could Do It!
Counting to 5

Keep little fingers busy with this adorable counting song! As you lead youngsters in singing the song, have each child put up each of the five fingers on one hand as he repeatedly counts to five. Then give congratulatory high fives at the end of the tune, and encourage youngsters to give them to one another as well!

(sung to the tune of "Bingo")

Can you count to five with me?
I know that you can do it!
1, 2, 3, 4, 5!
1, 2, 3, 4, 5!
1, 2, 3, 4, 5!
I knew that you could do it! *(Give high fives.)*

One, two, three!

Oh, What Fun!
Counting to 10

Youngsters count to ten on their fingers as they sing this lively tune!

(sung to the tune of the chorus of "Jingle Bells")

One, two, three,
Four, five, six,
Seven, eight, nine, ten!
Oh, what fun it is to count!
Let's do it once again! Oh…

"Berry" Good Counting
Counting to 20

Use the patterns on page 23 to make 20 red strawberry cutouts. Place a desired number of berries on a large paper plate or plate cutout; then lead students in chanting the verse below. Enlist student help in counting the strawberries. Then serve up a new helping of strawberries and repeat the activity.

Strawberries, strawberries, taste just great!
How many strawberries on the plate?

Blast Off!
Counting backward from 10 to 1

Little ones pose as rockets for this fingerplay.
Have each child put both hands over his head to form
the pointed tip of a rocket as he squats down on the
launchpad. After the countdown, have him blast off by
jumping up to a standing position!

A rocket sat on the launching pad,
Pointing toward the sun.
It knew the time to blast off would be
On the count of one.
10-9-8-7-6-5-4-3-2-1... Blast off!

Number Detectives
Recognizing and naming written numbers to 10

To prepare for this activity, use the pattern on page
24 to make a tagboard magnifying glass cutout for
each child. Teach students the song below, naming a
number in the last line. Then encourage youngsters to
look through their magnifying glasses and try to find the
named numeral somewhere in the classroom. Repeat with
different numbers as desired.

(sung to the tune of "Pawpaw Patch")

Can you be a number detective?
Can you be a number detective?
Can you be a number detective?
Look all around and find a [9]!

Can You Find It?
Recognizing written numbers to 10

Display a s... of number cards from 1 to 10 in sequential order. (Se... ...–107 for a set of cards.) Then lead student... ...e song below. At the end of the song, ask a... ...nteer to come up and point to the named... ...ng additional verses, substituting a different... ...time.

(...e tune of "The Muffin Man")

Can yo... ...umber [6],
The nu... ...e number [6]?
Can yo... ...number [6],
And p... ...r me?

Missing!
Identifying missing numbers to 10

In advance, gather a few sequential number cards. (See pages 103–107 for a set of cards.) Secretly conceal one number before displaying the other card... in sequence. To begin, teach little ones the song sho... Pause at the end of the song to have youngsters ide... the missing number. Next, present the missing car... invite a volunteer to put it in its proper place. The... the volunteer point to each number as the rest o... youngsters count aloud. To repeat the activity,... a new sequence of numbers (with one missing... the song again.

(sung to the tune of "The More We Ge...

There's a number missing!
It's missing, it's missing.
There's a number missing!
Oh, what can it be?

Out of Order
Ordering numbers to 10

Display in random order a set of three or four number cards like the ones on pages 103–107. Lead youngsters in singing the song below. After the final line, ask a student volunteer to place the number cards in sequential order. Then mix up the cards, sing again, and ask a different volunteer to set the numbers straight!

(sung to the tune of "The Wheels on the Bus")

All of these numbers are out of order,
Out of order, out of order.
All of these numbers are out of order.
Can you fix them, please?

Red or Pink?
Comparing sets to 10

Create a garden for this fingerplay by making ten red and ten pink construction paper copies of the flower patterns on page 25. Prepare them for flannelboard use. Place a set of red flowers on one half of the board and a set of pink flowers on the other half. Next, teach youngsters the fingerplay shown, counting each set of flowers. Then lead youngsters in determining which set has more.

Take a look at my garden.	Shade eyes with hand.
What do you see?	Shrug and put hands out, palms up.
Red flowers, pink flowers,	Point to each set.
Yes sirree!	Nod head.
Are there more red?	Point to the red flowers.
Are there more pink?	Point to the pink flowers.
Count them and tell me	
What you think!	Tap temple with index finger.

Nothing at All
Understanding the concept of zero

Reinforce the meaning of zero for your young students with this very simple tune!

(sung to the tune of "The Farmer in the Dell")

Nothing at all,	*Show empty hands.*
Nothing at all.	*Show empty hands.*
Heigh-ho, that is zero!	*Use both hands to form a 0.*
Nothing at all!	*Show empty hands.*

Special Number
Recognizing written numbers 11 to 20

For this small-group activity, place a set of number cards faceup on a table. (See pages 108–112 for a set of cards.) Tell youngsters that a special number is hiding somewhere among the cards and you need them to help you find it; then name the number. Select a volunteer and enlist student help in reciting the chant below, filling in the volunteer's name where indicated. Next, have the volunteer point to the special number. If she is correct, name a new number to begin another round of play. If the child does not find the special number, offer hints to help her find the desired card and then invite students to repeat the chant while she tries again.

Special number, are you near?
[Molly] will find you, never fear!

Sets of Stars
Matching sets to numerals

To prepare, use the patterns on page 25 to make ten yellow construction paper star cutouts. Then prepare them for flannelboard use. Place a set of one to ten stars on the board, and spread out a set of number cards nearby. (See pages 103–107 for a set of cards.) Lead youngsters in singing the song below. After the final line, count the stars together to determine the number in the set. Then ask a student volunteer to find the matching number card. Repeat the activity several times, changing the number of stars on the board each time.

(sung to the tune of "Row, Row, Row Your Boat")

Stars, stars, stars so bright!
How many can there be?
How many, how many, how many, how many,
How many do you see?

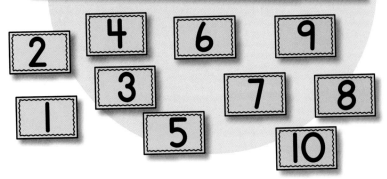

Looking Fine in Line
Identifying ordinal numbers

Invite five students to line up in front of your group, one behind another. Announce an ordinal number; then encourage the remainder of the class to observe the line and notice who is standing in that position. Next, enlist student help in singing the song shown. At the end of the song, ask a student volunteer to name the child in the indicated position. Repeat the song, substituting a different ordinal number until all five students have been named. Continue with different groups of five students as desired.

(sung to the tune of "Oh Where, Oh Where Has My Little Dog Gone?")

Oh who, oh who is the [first] child in line?
Oh who, oh who can it be?
Can you tell me the name of the [first] child in line?
Oh who, oh who can it be?

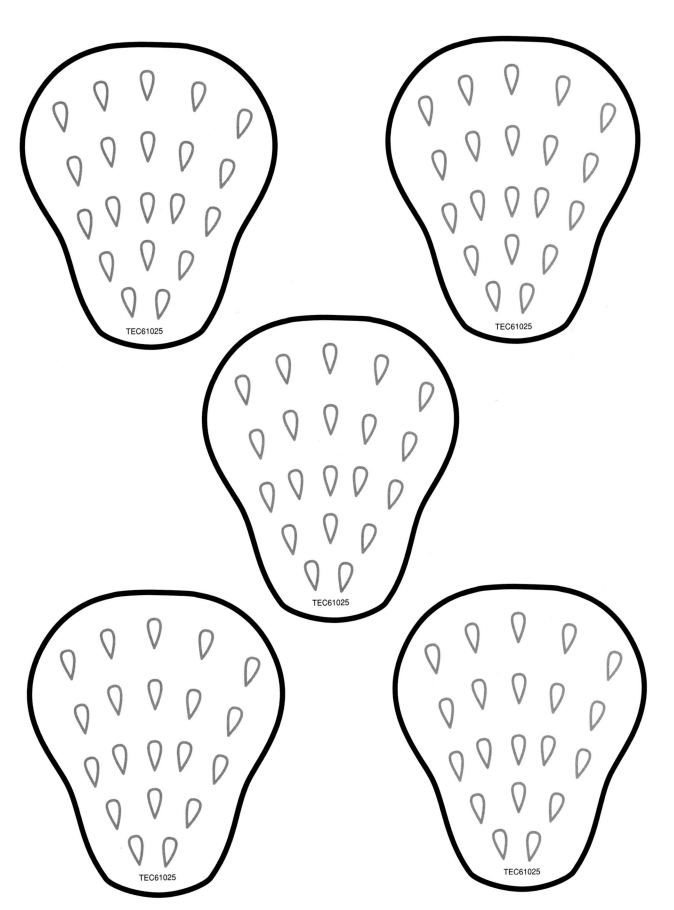

Magnifying Glass Pattern
Use with "Number Detectives" on page 18.

Cut here.

TEC61025

Flower Patterns
Use with "Red or Pink?" on page 20.

Star Patterns
Use with "Sets of Stars" on page 22.

Teddy Teatime
Understanding one-to-one correspondence

Serve up plenty of math at this imaginative center! Stock a center with a small table and four chairs, four teddy bears (or other stuffed animals), and sets of four plastic plates, cups, spoons, and napkins. Ask a student in this center to set the table for a bears' party. Explain that each bear will need one plate, one cup, one spoon, and one napkin. When the table is set, he seats the bears and begins the party!

Stamp, Stamp, Stamp
Counting to 3

This simple center provides plenty of colorful counting practice. Choose any three stamps from your rubber stamp collection and create a stamping sheet similar to the one shown. Then copy the sheet to make a class supply. Place the sheets, the corresponding rubber stamps, and ink pads in a center. Have each child count aloud as she stamps each design three times.

Dinosaur Spikes
Counting to 5

Preparing this prehistoric center is a snap! Make five tagboard copies of the spikeless stegosaurus pattern on page 35. Cut out the dinosaurs; then place them in a center with 25 colorful plastic clothespins. A student at this center clips five clothespins onto each dinosaur's back to give it spikes. To check his work, he recounts the spikes on each stegosaurus.

Ten Colorful Cookies
Counting to 10

Gourmet counting, anyone? Set up your play dough center with ten different cookie cutters, various colors of dough, rolling pins, and cookie sheets. Ask each young chef to roll out dough, cut one cookie with each cutter, and place it on her cookie sheet. When she has made one of each design, have her count the cookies. Then have her cut and count to ten all over again!

Seashells in the Sand
Counting to 20

This sandy center is almost as fun as a trip to the beach! Hide a collection of 20 craft foam seashells in your sand table. Place a sand pail and shovel nearby. A youngster visits the center and hunts for shells. When she has an assortment of shells in her pail, she stops and counts how many she has found. If she has found fewer than 20 shells, she hunts for more. If she has found all 20, she buries the shells for the next seeker.

Scarecrow's Patches
Recognizing and naming written numbers 1 to 10

For this teacher-directed center, first use the pattern on page 36 to make a class supply of white construction paper scarecrows. Then cut enough colorful construction paper "patches" so that each child will have at least ten. Working with one small group at a time, give each child a scarecrow pattern, a cotton swab, and access to a shallow container of glue. Direct each youngster to put a specific color patch on a specific number. For example, you might say, "Glue a red patch on the number three." You'll quickly see which children recognize their numerals, and you'll have a collection of cute scarecrow art when you're finished!

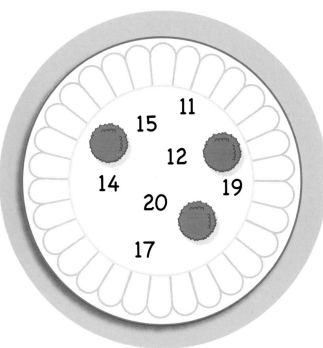

Bunches of Berries!

Recognizing and naming written numbers 11 to 20

This version of a lotto game is just "ripe" for a teacher-led center! In advance, randomly write the numbers 11 to 20 on each of four paper plates. Place the plates in a center with 40 large red or purple pom-poms to resemble berries. To play, call out a number between 11 and 20 as each youngster finds and covers it on her plate. Continue in this manner until each child has covered all her numbers and announces, "Bunches of berries!" Then spot-check each child's work by uncovering a number and asking her to name it. Play again if desired, making sure to call the numbers in a different order.

Build a Train

Ordering numbers to 10

This simple train provides plenty of number practice! Cut one square and 11 rectangles from colorful construction paper. Next, glue the square to a rectangle to resemble a train engine and decorate it as desired. Label each remaining rectangle with a different numeral from 1 to 10. Place the prepared pieces at a center. A student orders the rectangles from 1 to 10 to build a train.

Ducks in a Row
Ordering numbers to 20

Transform your water table into a ducky bubble bath! Use a permanent marker to label each of 20 craft foam duck cutouts (pattern on page 34) with a different numeral from 1 to 20. Add a squirt of mild bubble bath to the water in your water table and use an eggbeater or whisk to whip up a tub full of bubbles. Mix up the ducks and place them in the tub. Youngsters at this center find the ducks and stick them to the side of the water table, in order, from 1 to 20.

Something's Missing Here...
Identifying missing numbers to 10

Select four number cards with a sequence of consecutive numbers anywhere from 1 to 10. (See pages 103–107 for a set of cards.) Take one card out of the sequence and set it aside in a "reserve pile." Place the remaining cards in a large resealable plastic bag. Make a few more bags with incomplete card sequences inside. Then put the bags of cards and the reserve pile at a center. A child chooses a bag, lays out the cards, and determines which number is missing. Then she locates the needed number in the reserve pile. Once she completes the sequence, she removes one card from the set, places it in the reserve pile, and rebags the other cards. She continues with the other bags in this manner.

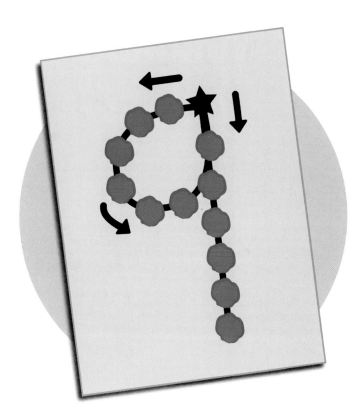

Dotted Digits
Writing numbers 1 to 10
To prepare, write a numeral from 1 to 10 on a sheet of paper. (You may wish to mark the starting point and stroke direction.) Then make a class supply of copies. Place the copies in a center along with several colorful bingo daubers. A child uses a marker to make dots along the lines of the numeral. Restock the center with each numeral, in turn, and encourage youngsters to dot more digits!

The Number Book
Writing numbers 1 to 10
Inside each of ten page protectors, slip a sheet of copy paper on which you've written a different number between 1 and 10. Place the sequenced pages in a three-ring binder. Put the binder in a center with a supply of colorful washable markers and a damp sponge. A child opens the binder and uses a marker to trace the number on each page. When she is finished, she wipes the marker from the page protectors to prepare the book for the next number writer!

Vroom! Vroom!
Forming numbers

All you need for this math center is masking tape and some toy cars! Use the masking tape to form any number or numbers from 11 to 20 on the floor in an open area of your room. Use a permanent marker to draw arrows on the tape to guide youngsters' number formation. Also provide a container of small toy cars. A child in this center drives the cars along the tape "road," following the arrows to form each number. Encourage older students to count to the number while they cruise along the roads.

Squeaky Clean Sets
Comparing sets

You may think of washing dishes as a chore, but your little ones will love it! Transform your water table into a kitchen sink with just a squirt of mild dishwashing soap. Then add some sturdy plastic plates, cups, and spoons. Place a couple of sponges and dishtowels nearby. A pair of students washes and dries the dishes and then places them on a nearby table. Next, the twosome compares the sets of plates, cups, and spoons. They decide which group has more and which has fewer. Youngsters count the number in each set and confirm their comparisons. Then they clear the table and put the dishes in the sink for the next pair of visitors.

Like Bees to a Flower
Matching sets to numerals

Youngsters will make a beeline to this center! To prepare, copy the patterns on page 37 on colorful tagboard; then cut the cards apart. Glue each bee to a clothespin as shown. Place the bees and flower cards in a center. A child chooses a card, counts the flowers, and then clips on the corresponding bee. He continues in this manner until he has matched each bee to its set of flowers.

Make Mine Pepperoni!
Matching sets to numerals

Serve up some pepperoni pizza at this center! Copy the pizza pattern on page 38 on tagboard to make ten copies. On one side of each pizza, write a different numeral from 1 to 10. On the other side, attach a corresponding set of red sticky dots. Next, cut the pizza in half. Store all the pieces in a bag and place it at a center. A child assembles each pizza by matching the dot set with the appropriate number.

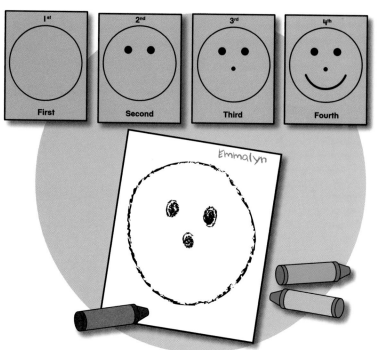

A Step-by-Step Happy Face!
Sequencing ordinal numbers

Smile! This cheerful center is a breeze to prepare!
Copy the sequencing cards on page 39 on tagboard.
Cut the cards apart, shuffle them, and place them at a
center with paper and crayons. A child first sequences
the cards to show how to draw a happy face step by
step. Once she has the cards in order, she follows the
directions to draw a happy face or two!

Duck Pattern
Use with "Ducks in a Row"
on page 30.

TEC61025

©The Mailbox® • *Numbers for Little Learners* • TEC61025

Note to the teacher: Use with "Scarecrow's Patches" on page 28.

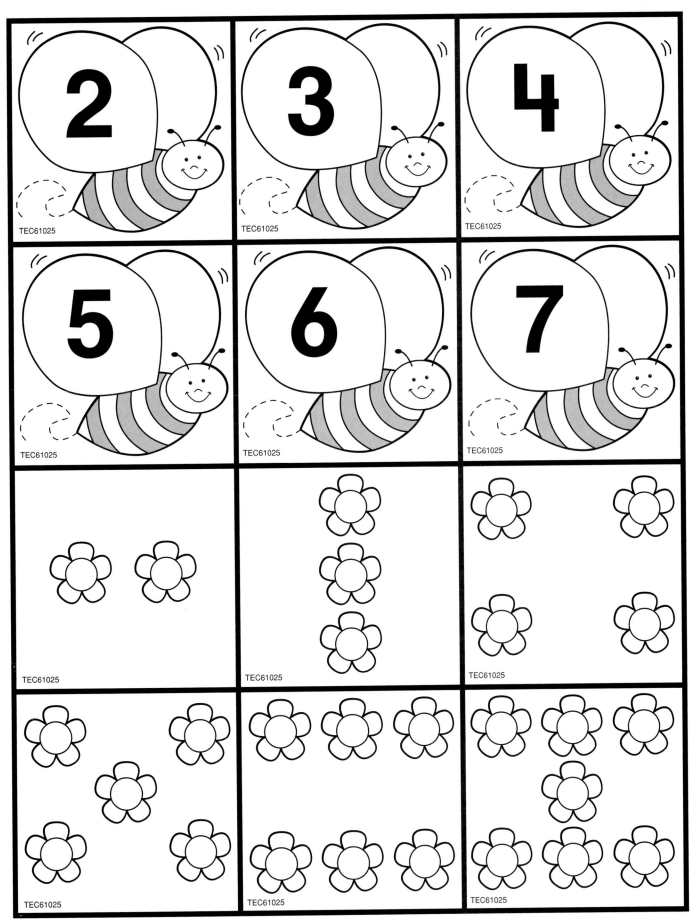

TEC61025

TEC61025

TEC61025

TEC61025

TEC61025

TEC61025

TEC61025

TEC61025

TEC61025

TEC61025

TEC61025

TEC61025

Pizza Pattern

Use with "Make Mine Pepperoni!" on page 33.

TEC61025

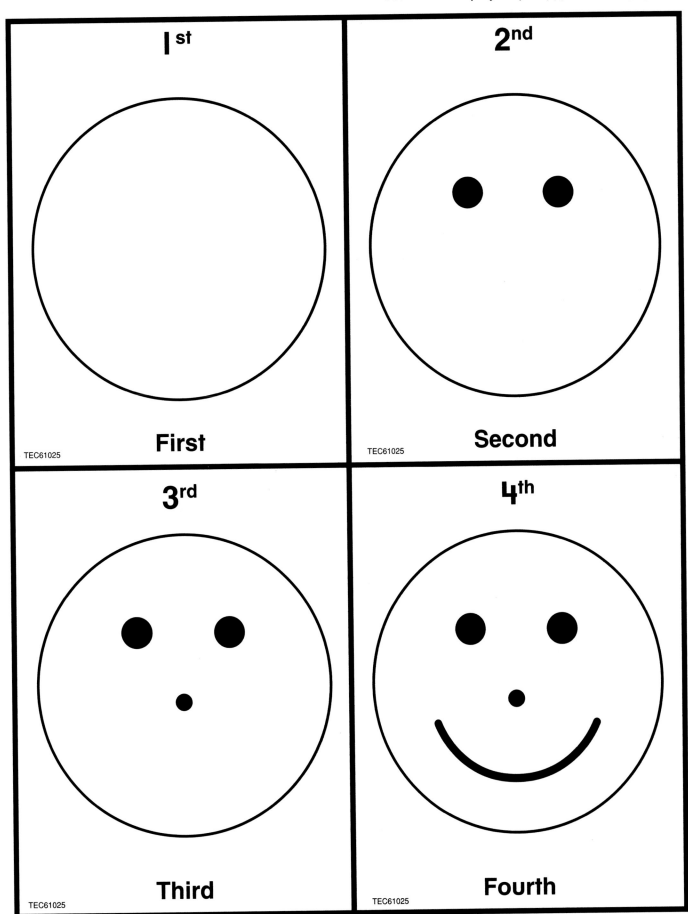

1st

First

TEC61025

2nd

Second

TEC61025

3rd

Third

TEC61025

4th

Fourth

TEC61025

Crunch, Crunch, Crunch
Understanding one-to-one correspondence

Give each child three crackers and three thin slices of cheese. Invite each child to look at her snack ingredients and decide if she has more, fewer, or the same number of cheese slices and crackers. Then ask her to check her prediction by using one-to-one correspondence to place one cheese slice on each cracker. One, two, three treats to eat!

Three!

1, 2, 3...Fruit Salad!
Counting to 3

Provide an assortment of fruit to make a healthy snack that's as easy as 1, 2, 3! Set out separate bowls of peeled apple slices, pineapple tidbits, and orange sections. (Or use other fresh or canned fruits that are easy for youngsters to handle in small pieces.) Give each child a small cup and a plastic spoon. Ask him to count out three of each type of fruit into his cup. When the counting's complete, encourage each child to stir up his personal fruit salad and enjoy!

Counting Cone
Counting to 5

The container for this snack tastes as good as what's inside! Set out separate bowls of small cheese-filled sandwich crackers, fish-shaped crackers, and O-shaped cereal. Give each child a flat-bottomed ice-cream cone. Direct each youngster to count five of each item into her ice-cream cone. Then invite her to eat this tasty mix— and the cone too!

S'more Mix
Counting to 20

Put the yummy taste of a s'more into a snack mix that's perfect for counting practice! Set out separate bowls of Golden Grahams cereal, chocolate chips, and vanilla chips. Give each child a small cup or plastic bag. Ask him to count 20 pieces of cereal, ten chocolate chips, and five vanilla chips into his container. Then invite everyone to munch their mix!

...three, two, one!

Eating Sand? Grand!
Counting backward from 10 to 1

Give each child a resealable plastic bag with two vanilla wafers sealed inside. Ask each child to use his hands to completely crush the cookies in his bag as the class slowly counts backward from 10 to 1. (If the cookies need to be more crumbled, have children continue to crush the cookies as they count back from 10 a second time.) Then give each child a serving of blue-tinted vanilla pudding. Have him sprinkle the crushed cookies over the pudding to resemble a sandy beach. Provide spoons and invite youngsters to eat their "beachy-keen" snacks!

Pass the Plates
Recognizing and naming numbers to 10

To prepare for this activity, write a numeral between 0 and 10 on each of a class supply of paper plates. At snacktime, distribute the plates. Ask each child to identify the number on her plate. Then play some lively music and have students pass their plates around the table. When you stop the music, ask each child to identify the number on the plate that she's holding. Continue in this manner for several rounds; then give each child a small cupful of O-shaped cereal. Encourage her to place the cereal along the lines of her plate's numeral before eating it!

Orderly Cookies
Ordering numbers to 5

For each child, place five vanilla wafers on a large plate. Use gel icing to write one numeral from 1 to 5 on each cookie; then mix them up so they are out of order. At snack time, ask each child to arrange his cookies in order from 1 to 5. After you check his work, invite him to eat the cookies in order. One, two, three, four, five—delicious!

Roll a Number
Forming numbers

These numbers are delicious! Give each child a length of refrigerated breadstick dough on a sheet of waxed paper. Have her roll the breadstick into a slightly longer snake shape and then form the dough into a numeral from 0 to 9. Challenge older preschoolers to form numerals from 10 to 20. Place the dough numbers on a cookie sheet; then bake as directed on the breadstick package. If desired, serve the cooled number breadsticks with a brush of melted butter.

Cinnamon Numbers
Forming numbers 11 to 20

This stay-fresh snack can be repeated as often as you like! Set out separate bowls of cinnamon graham cracker sticks and Apple Jacks cereal. Give each child a copy of a number card from pages 108–112 to use as a mat. Help each child identify her number and then ask her to cover the numerals with graham sticks and cereal pieces. Once a child has formed her number, invite her to eat the graham sticks and cereal.

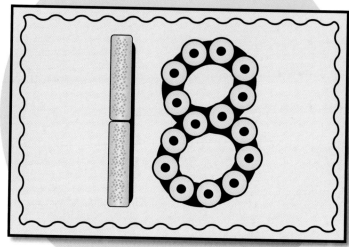

Something's Fishy!
Comparing sets

Mix together two bags of two distinctly different types of fish-shaped crackers, such as pretzel, graham, or cheddar cheese flavors. Give each child a small cup of cracker mix and a copy of the workmat on page 46. Ask him to sort the fish into the two fishbowls. Then have him compare the results. Do the bowls have the same number of fish? Which bowl has more fish? Which has fewer fish? After sorting and comparing, invite little ones to enjoy the catch of the day!

Whip Up a Number
Matching sets to numerals

This delicious snack combines number and set matching with number formation! Give each child a colorful paper plate and ten pretzel sticks. On each child's plate, use a can of whipped cream to form a numeral from 1 to 10. Then ask him to count out a corresponding number of pretzels to make a matching set. After checking for accuracy, have him use a pretzel to trace over the whipped cream numeral. Complete the activity by inviting youngsters to dip their pretzels into the whipped cream and munch away!

Cheery Cherry Lemonade
Sequencing ordinal numbers

Here's a sweet way to reinforce ordinal numbers! To prepare, color and cut apart the cards on a copy of page 47. Place the cards at a center with a small plastic pitcher of lemonade, a bowl of crushed ice cubes, and a container of the liquid drained from a large jar of maraschino cherries. Also stock the center with a class supply of clear plastic cups and spoons. Then help each child read the ordinal words to sequence the cards and follow the directions to prepare her own cup of delicious cherry lemonade.

1st	2nd	3rd	4th
First	Second	Third	Fourth

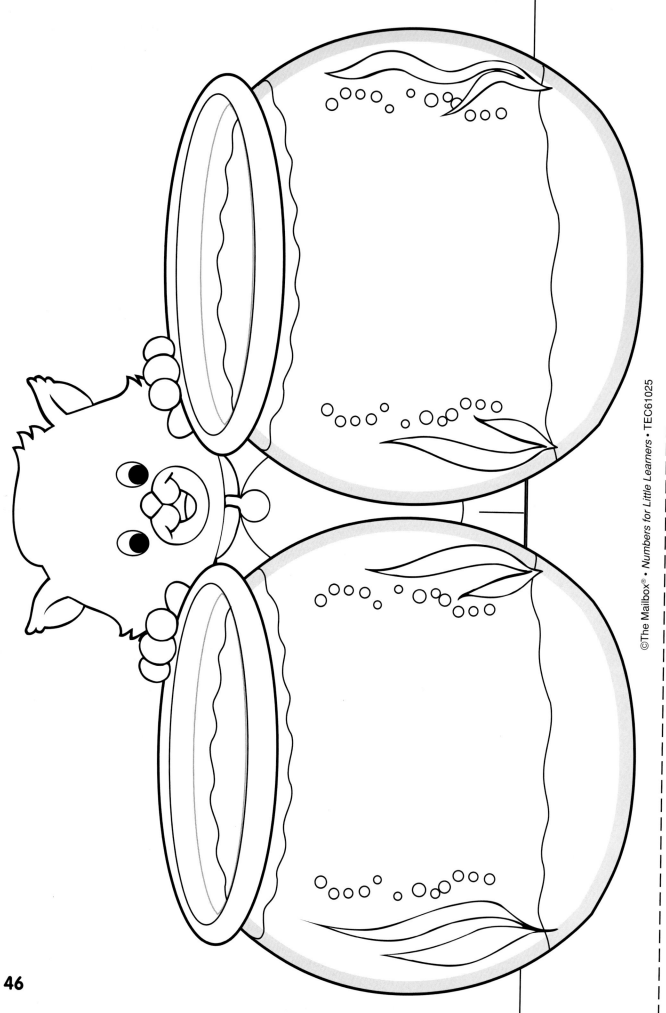

©The Mailbox® • *Numbers for Little Learners* • TEC61025

Note to the teacher: Use with "Something's Fishy!" on page 44.

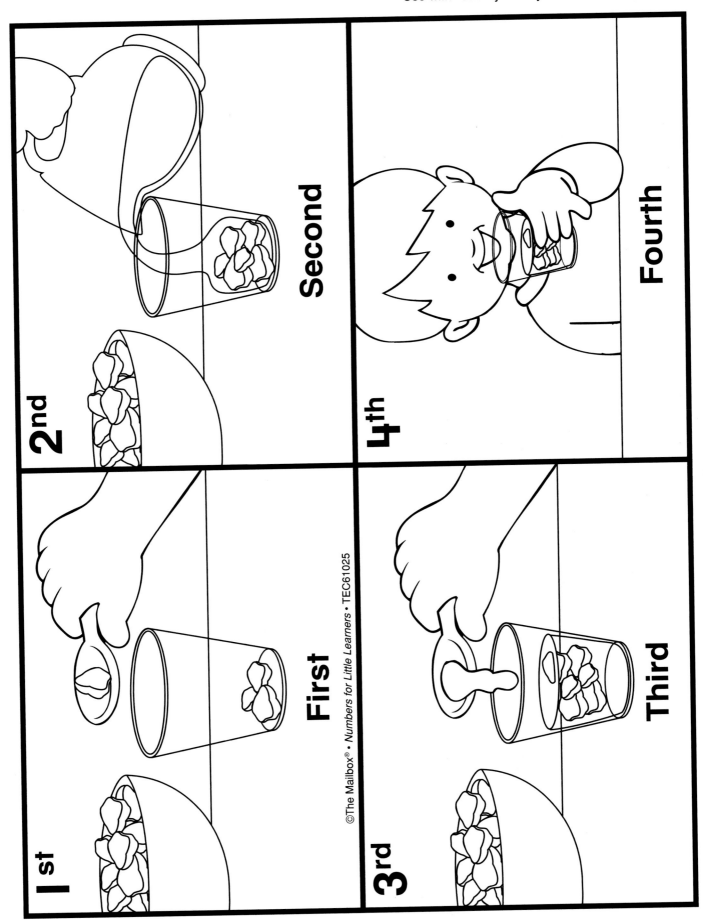

Second

2nd

Fourth

4th

First

1st

Third

3rd

©The Mailbox® • Numbers for Little Learners • TEC61025

Very Fine Vases
Understanding one-to-one correspondence

Little ones make sure each vase has a flower with this cute craft. To make a flower arrangement, a child glues three simple vase cutouts to a sheet of white construction paper as shown. Next, she draws one stem coming from the top of each vase. Then she glues one colorful flower cutout to the top of each stem. To complete the project, the child draws one leaf on each flower stem. Lead each child to conclude that there are the same number of vases, flowers, leaves, and stems.

Ants at a Picnic
Counting to 3

Youngsters count to three again and again as they create this picnic scene. To make one, a child glues a red paper semicircle to a sheet of construction paper. He then outlines the curved edge of the slice with green marker so it resembles a slice of watermelon. Next, he dips a finger into black tempera paint and makes three fingerprints on the watermelon slice to represent seeds. Then he prints three more black fingerprints (touching one another) to resemble an ant. He makes more ants on the paper as desired. When the paint is dry, he uses a fine-tip black marker to draw three legs on each side of each ant's body. For additional counting practice, have the child recount the body sections and legs on each ant.

Five Little Frogs
Counting to 5

These five little frogs are sure to charm youngsters! To prepare, use the frog pattern on page 57 to make five green construction paper frog cutouts per child. Also cut out a class supply of 18-inch brown construction paper logs. To make one project, a child first "speckles" the frogs and the log by dipping a toothbrush into green tempera paint. She rubs her thumb over the toothbrush bristles to flick paint over the frogs and log. Next, she repeats the process with brown paint. When the paint is dry, she adds facial features to the frogs. To complete the project, she counts the frogs on her finished artwork.

Butterflies in the Sky
Counting to 10

In advance, dye dry bow-tie pasta pieces a variety of colors so that there is enough for each child to have ten pieces, or collect ten butterfly stickers per child. Store the butterflies in a container. To make a butterfly sky, a youngster fringe-cuts one long edge of a 2" x 12" strip of green construction paper. He glues the resulting grass to one long side of a 9" x 12" sheet of blue construction paper to create a grass and sky background. Next, he counts out ten butterflies and glues them (or applies ten stickers) above the grass. When the glue is dry, he uses crayons to add details, such as a sun and clouds, to his picture. For added reinforcement, have him count his fancy fliers again.

Cotton Ball Clouds
Counting to 20

What can your little ones do with 20 cotton balls? Make these creative clouds, of course! In advance, gather enough cotton balls for each child to have 20 and place them in a container. To begin, a child takes 20 cotton balls and arranges them on a sheet of blue construction paper so that they resemble a large cloud. Next, she recounts the cotton balls as she glues each one in place. When the glue is dry, she uses a marker to draw an outline around the cloud. If desired, she writes or dictates to describe what shape or object her 20 cotton ball cloud resembles.

My cloud looks like a car.

Starry Night
Counting to 20

In advance, fold a 6" x 9" sheet of black construction paper lengthwise for each child. To make a starry-night scene, a student uses a star-shaped paper punch to punch three or four stars along the folded edge of the paper. Then he unfolds the paper and counts the stars. He continues punching stars around the edges of the paper until he has a total of 20. Next, he places a thin line of glue along the outer edges of a 6" x 9" sheet of aluminum foil. He glues the foil behind the black paper so that the stars shine through. Then he finishes the scene by using crayons to draw a moon. For additional counting practice, have the child recount his shiny stars.

Rocket Launch
Counting backward from 10 to 1

To prepare for liftoff, duplicate the rocket pattern on page 58 and the number cards on page 59 onto construction paper to make a class supply. Cut out the circle on each rocket pattern. To make one mobile, a child colors and cuts out a rocket pattern. With your help, she glues a small photo of herself behind the circle cutout and tapes a 30-inch length of yarn to the bottom back of the rocket. Next, she cuts out the number cards and places them in order, with the "1" card at the bottom and the "10" card at the top. After she tapes each number to the yarn, as shown, she holds the rocket and counts backward from 10 to 1. Blast off!

Goody, Goody, Gumballs!
Recognizing and naming written numbers 1 to 10

Mix art and assessment in this sweet small-group project! Give each child a white construction paper copy of the gumball machine pattern on page 60 and ask her to color its base. Then provide several different colors of bingo daubers. Announce a direction, such as "Make a red gumball on each number 4" or "Make a blue gumball on each number 8." Scan to determine each child's number recognition skills. Continue in this manner until students have filled their machines with colorful gumballs. For extra reinforcement, ask volunteers to name specific numerals as you point to them on a child's machine.

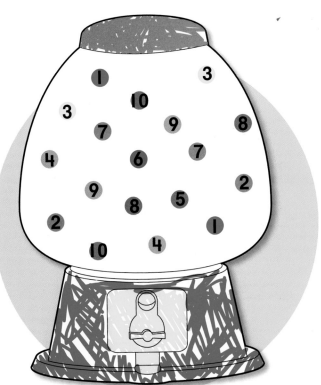

A House for Me
Recognizing and naming numbers 11 to 20

To prepare for this project, cut four two-inch white paper squares for each child. To make a house, a youngster glues a colorful construction paper square and triangle to a sheet of construction paper to resemble a house. Then she carefully tapes just the top of each square to represent windows on the house. She draws doors and other details as desired. To complete the project, take each child's house and write one number from 11 to 20 in random order behind each window. Return the youngster's house and encourage her to open each window and name the number. If desired, display the houses and encourage youngsters to peek under the windows and name each number.

Just Hangin' Out
Ordering numbers 1 to 5

In advance, draw a simple clothesline on a 6" x 18" sheet of construction paper for each child. To make one project, a child colors and cuts out a copy of the clothing patterns on page 61. Next, he orders the garments from 1 to 5 and glues them in sequence along the clothesline. He completes the project by drawing clothespins at the top of each garment. Then he checks his work by pointing to each number as he recounts the laundry.

Number Crowns
Ordering numbers 1 to 10

Your little ones can show off their number knowledge with these crowns! In advance, make a colorful construction paper copy of the appropriate crown pattern on page 62 for each child. To make a crown, a youngster cuts out the crown pattern and glues it to a sentence strip as shown. Then she stamps the numerals 1 to 10 in order along the strip, leaving space at each end. She uses craft supplies to embellish her crown as desired. Fit the strip around the child's head and tape the ends to secure it.

Nothing at All
Understanding the concept of zero

To prepare, cut a large number zero from white paper for each child. To make one project, each youngster fingerpaints in the color of his choice on a tabletop. He presses the zero cutout onto the painting to make a print, then lifts it off. When the paint is dry, he glues the colorful zero to a sheet of construction paper. Display the finished projects and encourage students to think of imaginative objects of which there are zero in the classroom, such as elephants or skyscrapers. Then list their dictation on a chart posted nearby.

In our classroom we have 0
gorillas
candy bars
dogs
bulldozers
cows
trees
dinosaurs

Just Noodling Around
Writing numbers 1 to 10

Cook up some fun when you invite youngsters to make numbers with noodles! In advance, boil a batch of spaghetti noodles and keep them wet as they cool. Also, program a sheet of construction paper with a desired number from 1 to 10 for each child. To make a noodle number, have a child follow the lines on her paper to form her number with wet spaghetti noodles. Provide additional noodles or help the child tear a noodle into a shorter piece as necessary. If desired, tape the paper's edges to a flat surface to dry overnight.

Rainbow Numbers
Writing numbers 1 to 10

These cheerful rainbows are sure to brighten your classroom! For each child, program a sheet of copy paper with a...

...within the outline until she is satisfied with the results. Then she mounts her rainbow number on a colorful sheet of construction paper.

Surprise!
Writing numbers 11 to 20

This activity is quite revealing! A child uses a white crayon to write three different numerals from 11 to 20 anywhere on a sheet of white paper. Then he exchanges papers with a classmate. Next, he uses watercolors to paint the entire paper, revealing the three surprise numbers. For an added challenge, invite youngsters to identify each number.

Bubbles, Bubbles
Comparing sets

Something's fishy in this activity! In advance, use the fish patterns on page 59 to make two colorful paper fish cutouts for each child. To make one project, a child glues the two fish on a sheet of blue construction paper. Then she glues a desired number of cereal rings above each fish to represent bubbles. When the glue is dry, she compares the sets of bubbles to determine which fish has more and which has fewer.

Octopus's Arms
Matching sets to numerals

This adorable octopus provides plenty of math practice! In advance, cut out for each child a large octopus head and body from a sheet of colorful 9" x 12" construction paper. Randomly program the bottom of each octopus cutout with eight numbers appropriate for your students. Next, for each child, cut a sheet of copy paper into eight one-inch strips. To make an octopus, a child uses markers to draw a face on a cutout. Then she tapes one strip below a numeral and uses a bingo dauber to make the corresponding dot set. She continues in this manner until each numeral has a corresponding dot set and the octopus has eight arms.

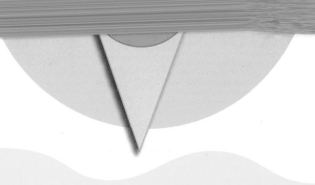

Here's the Scoop...
Identifying ordinal numbers

This yummy-looking, sweet-smelling project begins with scented paint. To prepare, add vanilla extract to white tempera paint, cocoa powder to brown paint, and

cone cutout. Then have her point to each scoop as you ask, "Which flavor did you put on the cone first? Second? Third?" Program the scoops with matching ordinal numbers to complete each child's cone.

TEC61025

TEC61025

TEC61025

TEC61025

TEC61025

Rocket Pattern

Use with "Rocket Launch" on page 51.

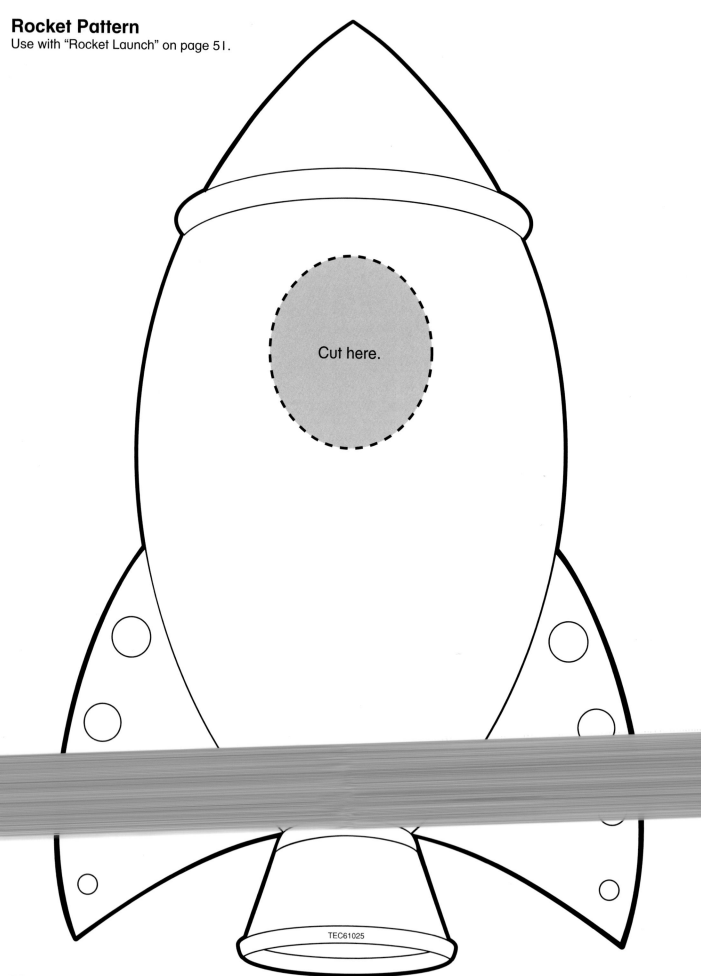

Cut here.

TEC61025

10	9	8	7	6
TEC61025	TEC61025	TEC61025	TEC61025	TEC61025
5	4	3	2	1
TEC61025	TEC61025	TEC61025	TEC61025	TEC61025

Fish Patterns
Use with "Bubbles, Bubbles" on page 55.

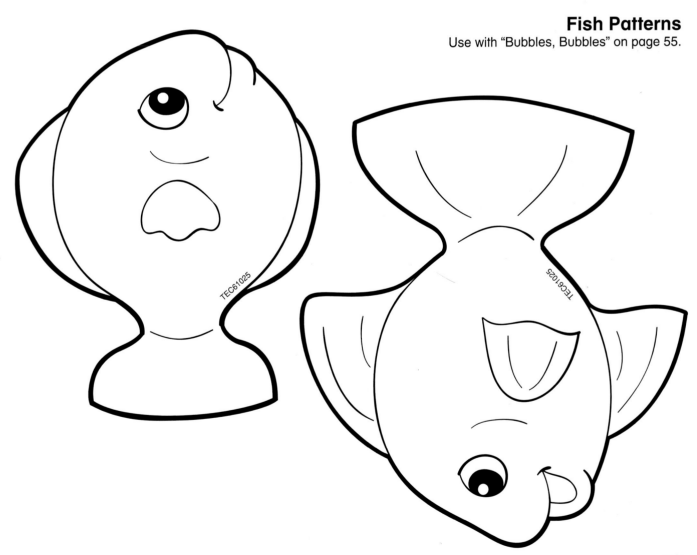

Gumball Machine Pattern
Use with "Goody, Goody, Gumballs!" on page 51.

1   3
10
3
7   9   8
4   7
6
2
9
8   5
2   1
10   4

TEC61025

TEC61025

2

4

TEC61025

3

TEC61025

1

5

TEC61025

TEC61025

King and Queen Crown Patterns

Use with "Number Crowns" on page 53.

Counting Queen

TEC61025

Counting King

TEC61025

For further number sense reinforcement, check out the eight reproducible booklets on pages 64–92. Use the directions below to assist each child in completing her booklet. Encourage youngsters to take their booklets home for further reinforcement.

How to Make the Booklets

Number Awareness

Follow the directions on page 64.

Counting to 5 • Writing Numbers to 10
pages 68–70   pages 87–92

Cut out a copy of the booklet cover and pages. Stack the pages in order behind the cover and then staple them along the left side. As you read aloud each page, have each child color or trace to complete the booklet.

Counting to 10 • Counting to 12
pages 71–73   pages 74–76

Copy and cut out the booklet pages and backing. Stack the pages in order and then staple them atop the backing page where indicated. As you read aloud each page, have each child count the featured item(s) and color the page as desired.

Counting to 20 • Counting Backward
pages 77–79   pages 80–82

Copy and cut out the booklet pages. Sequence and glue the pages as indicated. When the glue is dry, accordion-fold the booklet. As you read aloud each page, have each child count the featured item. After reading, invite her to color the booklet as desired.

Comparing Sets

Follow the directions on page 83.

Numbers Everywhere!

Pages 64–67

This booklet will remind youngsters of the many places they encounter numbers every day! To prepare, duplicate the booklet cover below and the booklet pages on pages 65–67 for each child. Cut apart the pages and stack them in order behind the booklet cover. Staple the booklet pages together along the left side. Then, as you read each page aloud, have each student complete the page as directed below.

Cover: Color the numbers. Write your name on the line.

Page 1: Color and decorate the cake.

Page 2: Draw hands on the clock.

Page 3: Color the shirt.

Page 4: Color the blocks.

Page 5: Color the number on the sign.

Page 6: Write numbers in the open space.

- -

Booklet Cover
Use with the directions on this page.

Number awareness

Numbers Everywhere!

10

8

3

Name _____

A number on a birthday cake.

1

Numbers on a clock.

2

Booklet Pages 3 and 4
Use with the directions on page 64.

Number awareness

A number on a great big shirt.

3

Numbers on my blocks.

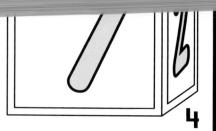

4

Number awareness

Booklet Pages 5 and 6
Use with the directions on page 64.

A number on a sign that's square.

5

Numbers, numbers everywhere!

6

Booklet Cover and Page 1
Use with the directions on page 63.

Counting to 5

Five in the Nest

Name _____

1 baby bird says, "Tweet!"

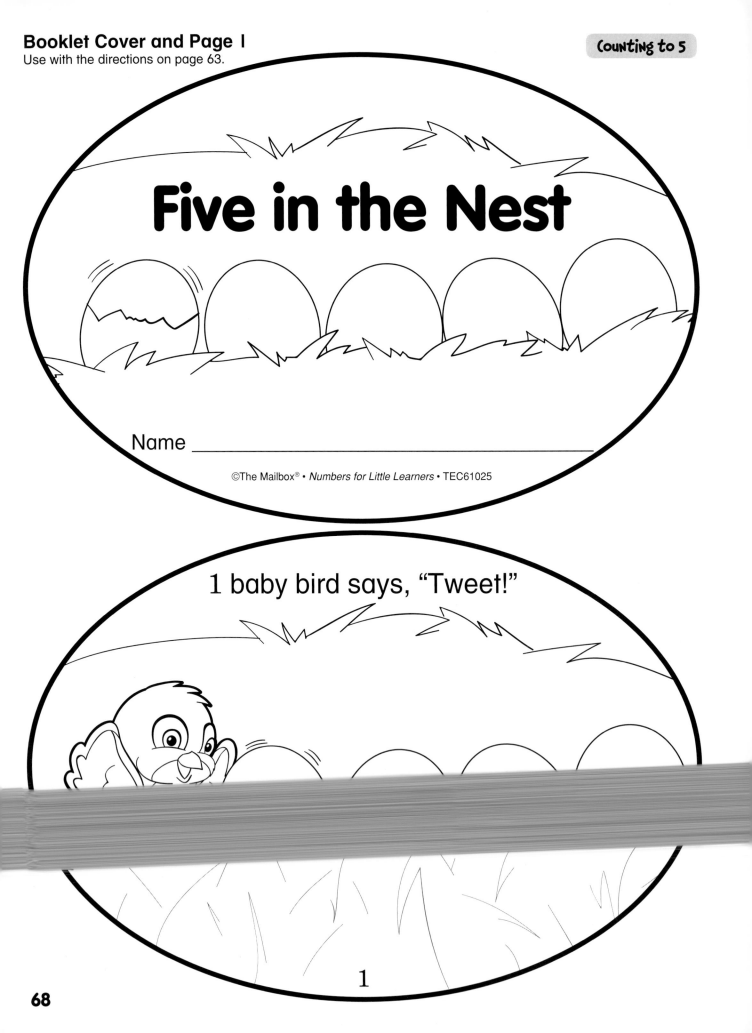

1

2 baby birds, how sweet!

2

3 baby birds, so neat!

3

Booklet Pages 4 and 5
Use with the directions on page 63.

Counting to 5

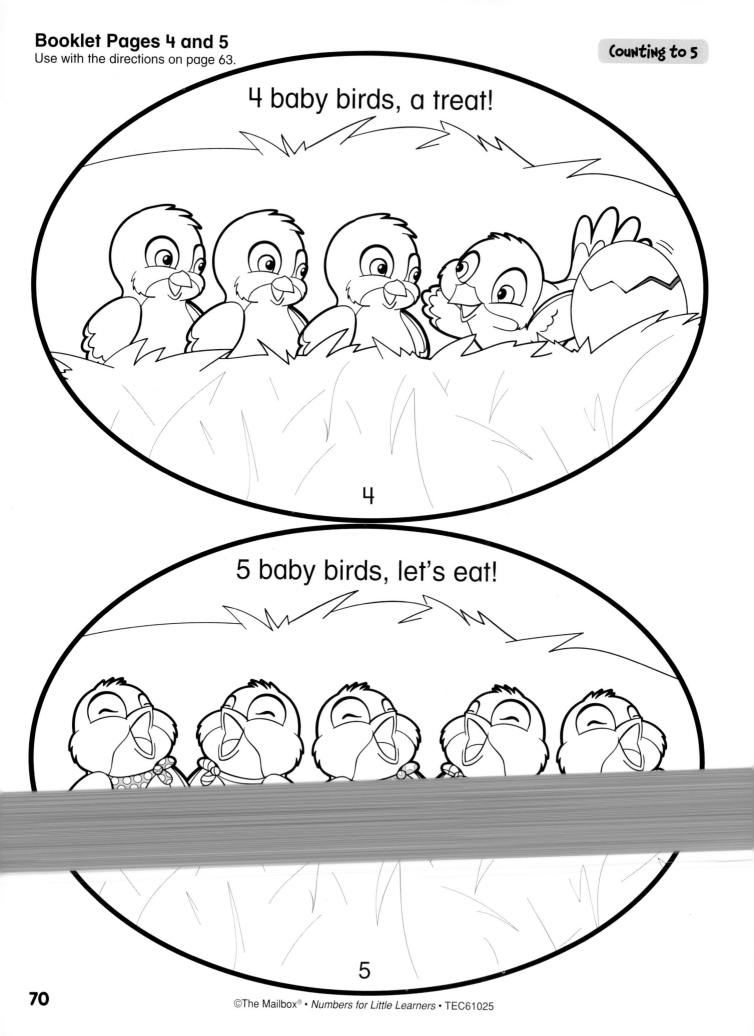

4 baby birds, a treat!

4

5 baby birds, let's eat!

5

Count to 10 Again and Again!

Draw 10 balloons.

Staple here.

5

Name _____

10 fingers and 10 toes.

1

10 flowers in a row.

2

10 cats in 10 hats.

3

10 worms, wiggly and fat.

4

3 cookies

6 cookies

4 cookies

cookies

cookies

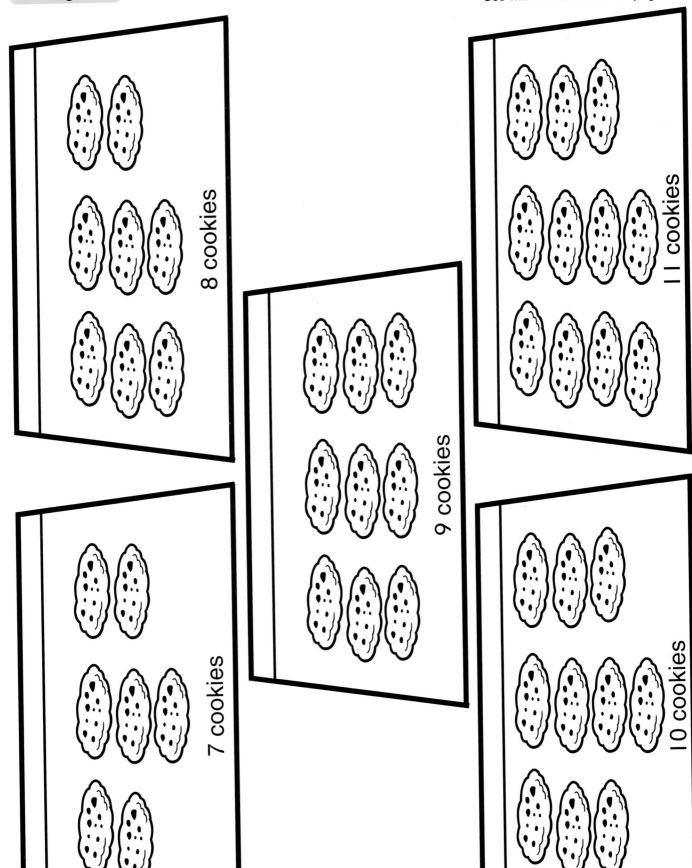

8 cookies

11 cookies

9 cookies

7 cookies

10 cookies

Booklet Backing and Page
Use with the directions on page 63.

Counting to 12

We want cookies.

It's time to bake.

How many cookies

will we make?

Staple here.

12 cookies

Name _____

©The Mailbox® • *Numbers for Little Learners* • TEC61025

I cookie

Counting to 20

Booklet Cover and Page 1
Use with the directions on page 63.

Counting Cars

Name _____

©The Mailbox® • *Numbers for Little Learners* • TEC61025

Glue page 1 here.

Cars on the highway?
There are plenty!
Count them now
From 1 to 20!

Glue page 2 here.

1

Glue page 5 here.

REPTILE FARM

4

EXIT ➡

5

Booklet Cover and Page 1
Use with the directions on page 63.

Counting backward

Sheep for Sleep

Name _____

Glue page 1 here.

It is time to go to sleep
Since the day is done.
Read along and count the sheep
From 10 down to 1.

e page 2 here.

1

Counting backward

Booklet Pages 2 and 3
Use with the directions on page 63.

Glue page 3 here.

2

Glue page 4 here.

3

Glue page 5 here.

4

5

©The Mailbox® • *Numbers for Little Learners* • TEC61025

Count and Compare!

Pages 83–86

To prepare, duplicate the booklet pages below and on pages 84–86 for each child. Cut out the pages and backing. Help each child compare the sets of strawberries on the backing. Lead him to conclude that the set that shows more strawberries is on the left side, while the set showing fewer is on the right. Next, invite each child to sort the booklet pages according to similar fruits. Then assist as needed as the child compares each pair of booklet pages, placing on the left side of the backing the page with the set showing more and on the right side the page with the set showing fewer. Have him continue in this manner until the pages are sorted. Then staple them in place on the backing. To complete the booklet, invite the child to color the pages as desired. Then read the booklet together, comparing each set of tasty fruits.

Comparing sets

Booklet Pages
Use with the directions above.

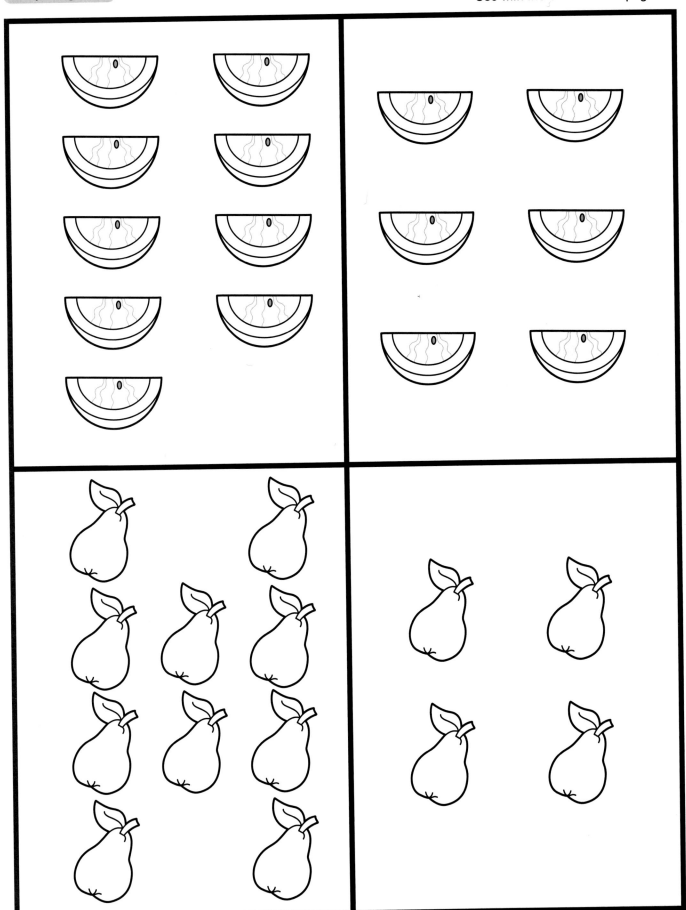

Staple here.

This set has **fewer**.

This set has **more**.

Name _____

©The Mailbox® • *Numbers for Little Learners* • TEC61025

nt and Compare!

Writing Numbers to 10

Booklet Cover and Page 1
Use with the directions on page 63.

You can write the numbers in this book!

Turn the page and take a look.

Read each poem and follow each line.

You'll write numbers that look so fine!

—

I Can Write Numbers!

Name _____

Booklet Pages 2 and 3
Use with the directions on page 63.

Writing Numbers to 10

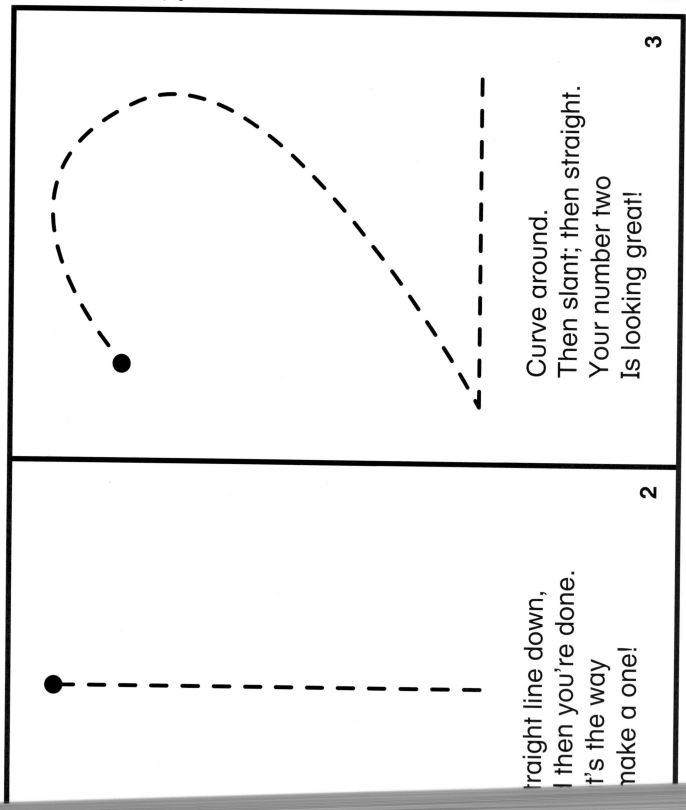

3

Curve around.
Then slant; then straight.
Your number two
Is looking great!

2

raight line down,
then you're done.
t's the way
ake a one!

©The Mailbox® • *Numbers for Little Learners* • TEC61025

Writing Numbers to 10

Booklet Pages 4 and 5
Use with the directions on page 63.

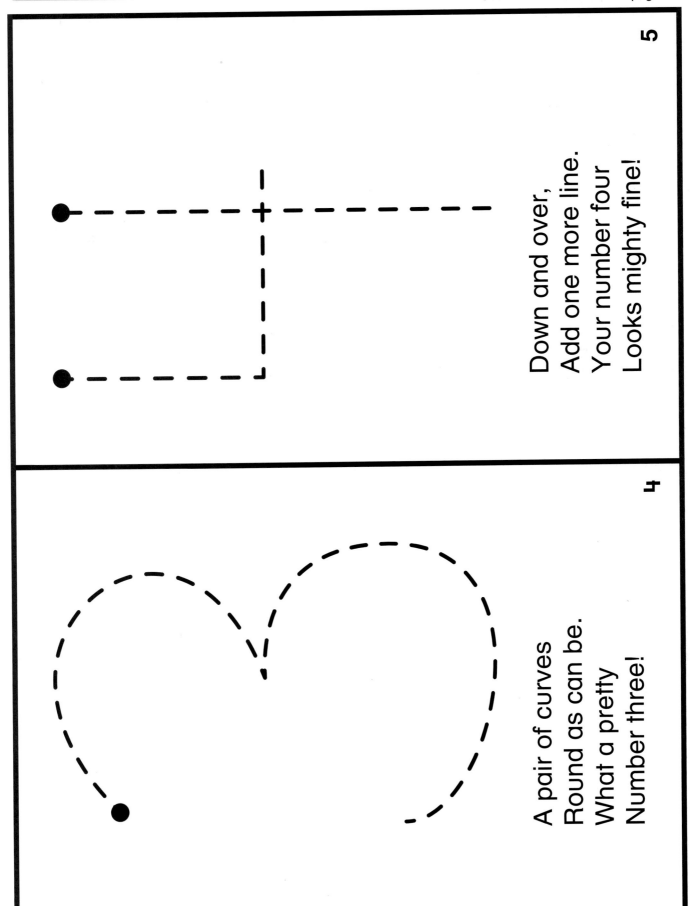

5

Down and over,
Add one more line.
Your number four
Looks mighty fine!

4

A pair of curves
Round as can be.
What a pretty
Number three!

Booklet Pages 6 and 7
Use with the directions on page 63.

Writing Numbers to 10

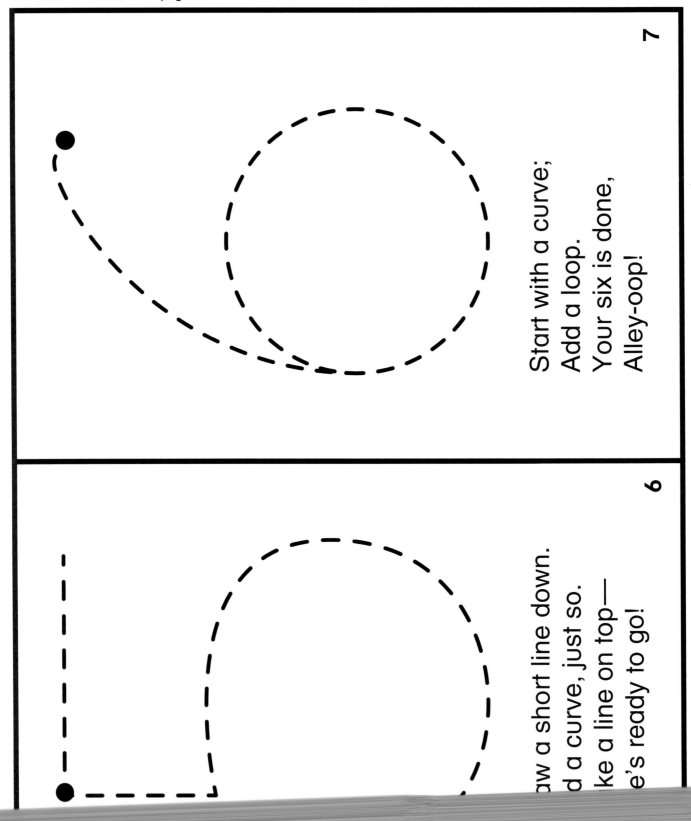

7

Start with a curve;
Add a loop.
Your six is done,
Alley-oop!

6

aw a short line down.
d a curve, just so.
ke a line on top—
e's ready to go!

Writing Numbers to 10

Booklet Pages 8 and 9
Use with the directions on page 63.

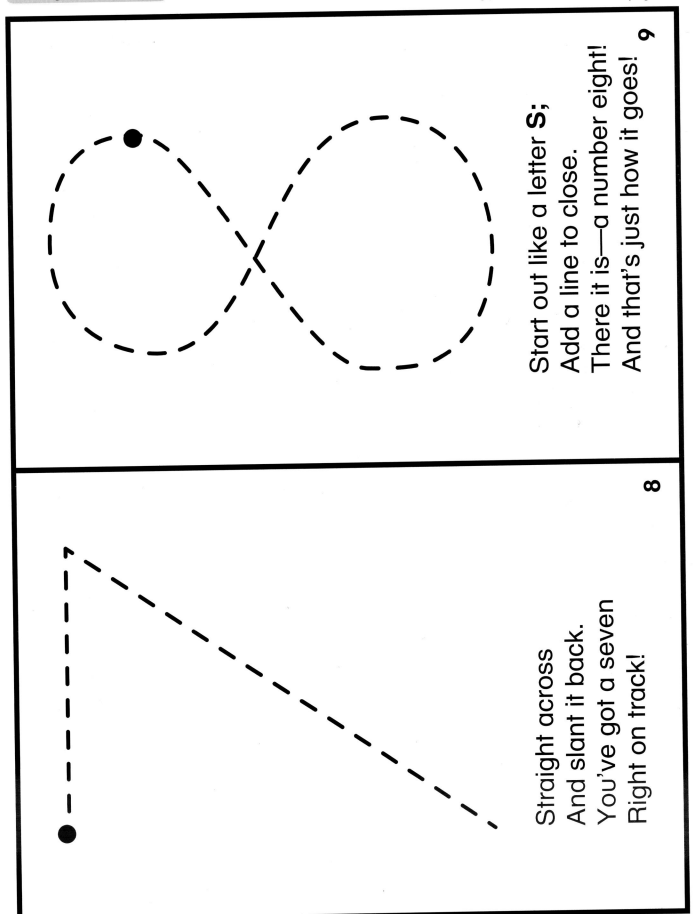

9

Start out like a letter **S**;
Add a line to close.
There it is—a number eight!
And that's just how it goes!

8

Straight across
And slant it back.
You've got a seven
Right on track!

Booklet Pages 10 and 11
Use with the directions on page 63.

Writing Numbers to 10

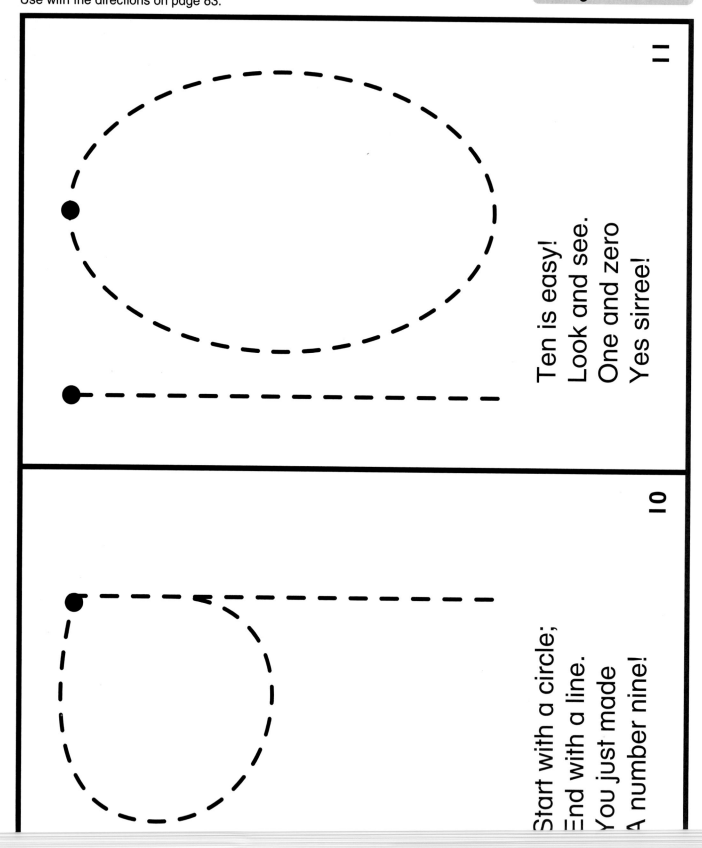

11

Ten is easy!
Look and see.
One and zero
Yes sirree!

10

Start with a circle;
End with a line.
You just made
A number nine!

Name _____

l one

|

Color l.

◯◯◯◯◯

Circle each l.

l	**2**
5	
9	**l**

l

l

Draw l.

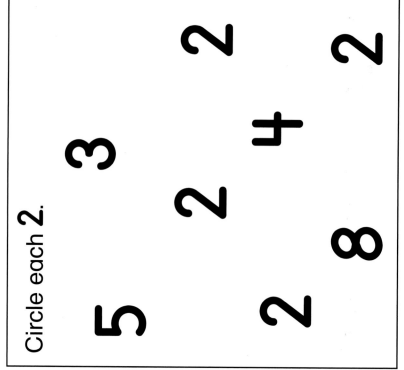

2 two

2

Circle each 2.

5   2   3

2   8   4   2

2

Co

Dr

94

©The Mailbox® • *Numbers for Little Learners* • TEC61025

Name _____

3 three

3 3

Circle each 3.

6

3

3

3

4

9

8

9

3

Color 3.

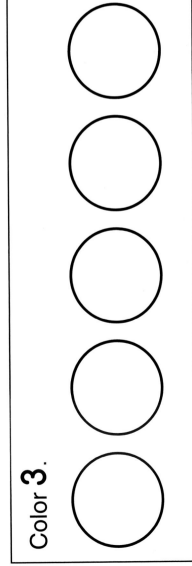

Draw 3.

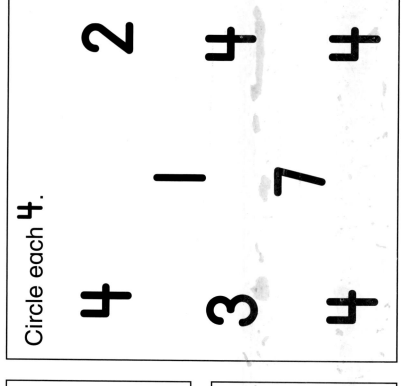

4 four

4

Circle each 4.

4	2
3	1
4	7
	4

©The Mailbox® • *Numbers for Little Learners* • TEC61025

Name _____

5 five

5 5 5

Color 5.

○ ○ ○ ○ ○

Draw 5.

Circle each 5.

5   2   5

6   7

3   5

97

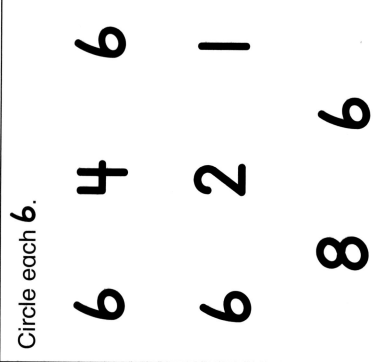

6 six

6

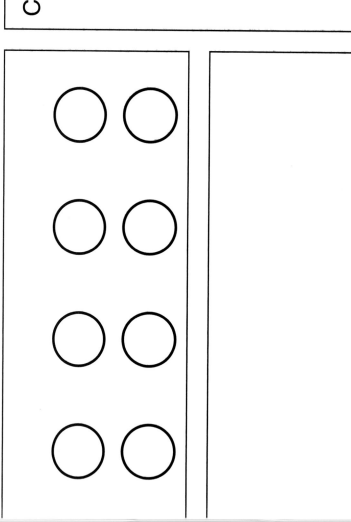

6	4	6
6	2	8
6	1	6

C

Dr

98

Name _____

7 seven

7

Circle each 7.

8	7	2
7	3	7
7	1	7

Color 7.

○ ○ ○ ○
○ ○ ○ ○

Draw 7.

8 eight

Circle each 8.

9   1   8

8   2   8

   6   8

C

D

Name _____

9 nine

9 9

Circle each 9.

6   1

9   5   9

9   4   9

Color 9.

○ ○ ○ ○ ○

○ ○ ○ ○

Draw 9.

10 ten

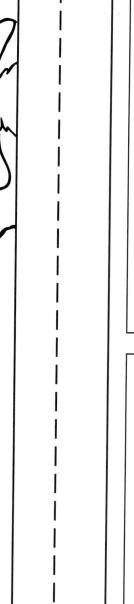

10

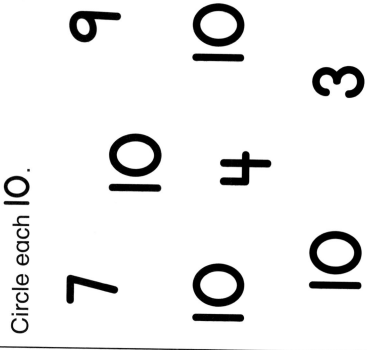

Circle each 10.

7   10   10

10   4   3

10   10   10

TEC61025

TEC61025

TEC61025

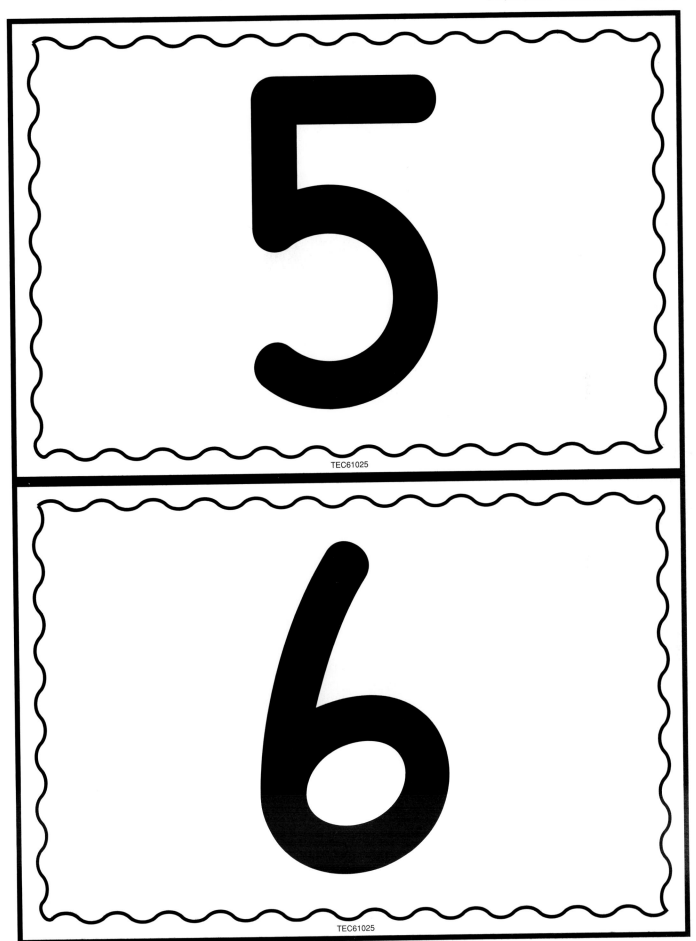

TEC61025

TEC61025

TEC61025

TEC61025

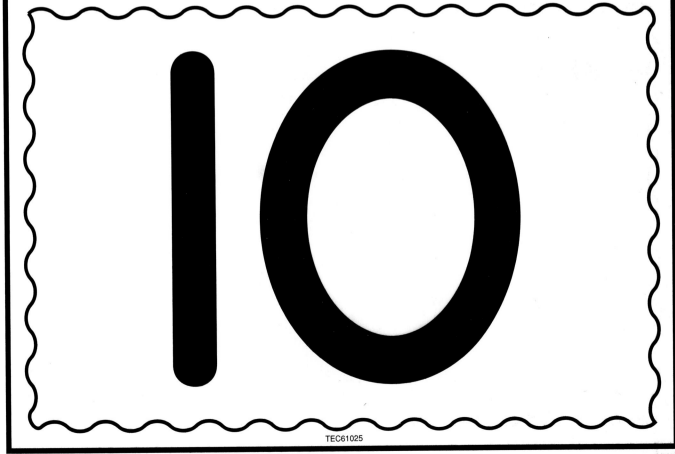

TEC61025

TEC61025

TEC61025

TEC61025

TEC61025

TEC61025

TEC61025

©The Mailbox® • *Numbers for Little Learners* • TEC61025

TEC61025

TEC61025

TEC61025

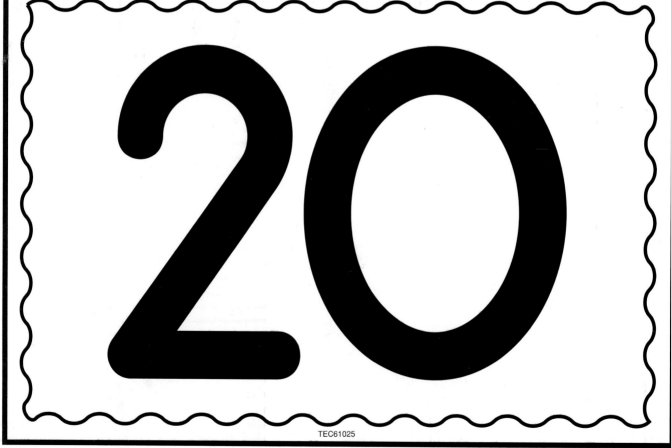

TEC61025